COLLECTED POEMS

ANNE BRONTË

This work is derived from the 1850 edition of the *Poems by Currer, Ellis, and Acton Bell*, published by Smith & Elder and edited by Charlotte Brontë, and is in the public domain. No copyright claim is made with respect to public domain works.

This edition contains minor editorial revisions to the original work.

CONTENTS

1. A Reminiscence — 1
2. The Arbour — 3
3. Home — 5
4. Vanitas Vanitatum, Omnia Vanitas — 7
5. The Penitent — 10
6. Music On Christmas Morning — 11
7. Stanzas — 14
8. If This Be All — 16
9. Memory — 18
10. To Cowper — 21
11. The Doubter's Prayer — 24
12. A Word To The "Elect." — 27
13. Past Days — 30
14. The Consolation — 32
15. Lines Composed in a Wood on a Windy Day — 34
16. Views Of Life — 36
17. Appeal — 45
18. The Student's Serenade — 46
19. The Captive Dove — 49
20. Self-Congratulation — 51
21. Fluctuations — 54
22. Despondency — 57
23. A Prayer — 59
24. In Memory of a Happy Day in February — 61
25. Confidence — 64
26. Lines Written From Home — 66
27. The Narrow Way — 68
28. Domestic Peace — 71
29. The Three Guides — 73
30. I hoped, that with the brave and strong — 83

A REMINISCENCE

Yes, thou art gone! and never more
Thy sunny smile shall gladden me;
But I may pass the old church door,
And pace the floor that covers thee,

May stand upon the cold, damp stone,
And think that, frozen, lies below
The lightest heart that I have known,
The kindest I shall ever know.

Yet, though I cannot see thee more,
'Tis still a comfort to have seen;
And though thy transient life is o'er,
'Tis sweet to think that thou hast been;

To think a soul so near divine,
Within a form so angel fair,
United to a heart like thine,
Has gladdened once our humble sphere.

THE ARBOUR

I'll rest me in this sheltered bower,
And look upon the clear blue sky
That smiles upon me through the trees,
Which stand so thick clustering by;

And view their green and glossy leaves,
All glistening in the sunshine fair;
And list the rustling of their boughs,
So softly whispering through the air.

And while my ear drinks in the sound,
My winged soul shall fly away;
Reviewing lone departed years
As one mild, beaming, autumn day;

And soaring on to future scenes,

Like hills and woods, and valleys green,
All basking in the summer's sun,
But distant still, and dimly seen.

Oh, list! 'tis summer's very breath
That gently shakes the rustling trees—
But look! the snow is on the ground—
How can I think of scenes like these?

'Tis but the FROST that clears the air,
And gives the sky that lovely blue;
They're smiling in a WINTER'S sun,
Those evergreens of sombre hue.

And winter's chill is on my heart—
How can I dream of future bliss?
How can my spirit soar away,
Confined by such a chain as this?

HOME

How brightly glistening in the sun
The woodland ivy plays!
While yonder beeches from their barks
Reflect his silver rays.

That sun surveys a lovely scene
From softly smiling skies;
And wildly through unnumbered trees
The wind of winter sighs:

Now loud, it thunders o'er my head,
And now in distance dies.
But give me back my barren hills
Where colder breezes rise;

Where scarce the scattered, stunted trees

Can yield an answering swell,
But where a wilderness of heath
Returns the sound as well.

For yonder garden, fair and wide,
With groves of evergreen,
Long winding walks, and borders trim,
And velvet lawns between;

Restore to me that little spot,
With gray walls compassed round,
Where knotted grass neglected lies,
And weeds usurp the ground.

Though all around this mansion high
Invites the foot to roam,
And though its halls are fair within—
Oh, give me back my HOME!

VANITAS VANITATUM, OMNIA VANITAS

In all we do, and hear, and see,
Is restless Toil and Vanity.
While yet the rolling earth abides,
Men come and go like ocean tides;

And ere one generation dies,
Another in its place shall rise;
THAT, sinking soon into the grave,
Others succeed, like wave on wave;

And as they rise, they pass away.
The sun arises every day,
And hastening onward to the West,
He nightly sinks, but not to rest:

Returning to the eastern skies,

Again to light us, he must rise.
And still the restless wind comes forth,
Now blowing keenly from the North;

Now from the South, the East, the West,
For ever changing, ne'er at rest.
The fountains, gushing from the hills,
Supply the ever-running rills;

The thirsty rivers drink their store,
And bear it rolling to the shore,
But still the ocean craves for more.
'Tis endless labour everywhere!
Sound cannot satisfy the ear,

Light cannot fill the craving eye,
Nor riches half our wants supply,
Pleasure but doubles future pain,
And joy brings sorrow in her train;

Laughter is mad, and reckless mirth—
What does she in this weary earth?
Should Wealth, or Fame, our Life employ,
Death comes, our labour to destroy;

To snatch the untasted cup away,
For which we toiled so many a day.

What, then, remains for wretched man?
To use life's comforts while he can,

Enjoy the blessings Heaven bestows,
Assist his friends, forgive his foes;
Trust God, and keep His statutes still,
Upright and firm, through good and ill;

Thankful for all that God has given,
Fixing his firmest hopes on Heaven;
Knowing that earthly joys decay,
But hoping through the darkest day.

THE PENITENT

I mourn with thee, and yet rejoice
That thou shouldst sorrow so;
With angel choirs I join my voice
To bless the sinner's woe.

Though friends and kindred turn away,
And laugh thy grief to scorn;
I hear the great Redeemer say,
"Blessed are ye that mourn."

Hold on thy course, nor deem it strange
That earthly cords are riven:
Man may lament the wondrous change,
But "there is joy in heaven!"

MUSIC ON CHRISTMAS MORNING

Music I love—but never strain
Could kindle raptures so divine,
So grief assuage, so conquer pain,
And rouse this pensive heart of mine—
As that we hear on Christmas morn,
Upon the wintry breezes borne.

Though Darkness still her empire keep,
And hours must pass, ere morning break;
From troubled dreams, or slumbers deep,
That music KINDLY bids us wake:
It calls us, with an angel's voice,
To wake, and worship, and rejoice;

To greet with joy the glorious morn,
Which angels welcomed long ago,
When our redeeming Lord was born,
To bring the light of Heaven below;
The Powers of Darkness to dispel,
And rescue Earth from Death and Hell.

While listening to that sacred strain,
My raptured spirit soars on high;
I seem to hear those songs again
Resounding through the open sky,
That kindled such divine delight,
In those who watched their flocks by night.

With them I celebrate His birth—
Glory to God, in highest Heaven,
Good-will to men, and peace on earth,
To us a Saviour-king is given;
Our God is come to claim His own,
And Satan's power is overthrown!

A sinless God, for sinful men,
Descends to suffer and to bleed;
Hell MUST renounce its empire then;
The price is paid, the world is freed,
And Satan's self must now confess
That Christ has earned a RIGHT to bless:

Now holy Peace may smile from heaven,
And heavenly Truth from earth shall spring:
The captive's galling bonds are riven,
For our Redeemer is our king;
And He that gave his blood for men
Will lead us home to God again.

STANZAS

Oh, weep not, love! each tear that springs
In those dear eyes of thine,
To me a keener suffering brings
Than if they flowed from mine.

And do not droop! however drear
The fate awaiting thee;
For MY sake combat pain and care,
And cherish life for me!

I do not fear thy love will fail;
Thy faith is true, I know;
But, oh, my love! thy strength is frail
For such a life of woe.

Were 't not for this, I well could trace
(Though banished long from thee)
Life's rugged path, and boldly face
The storms that threaten me.

Fear not for me—I've steeled my mind
Sorrow and strife to greet;
Joy with my love I leave behind,
Care with my friends I meet.

A mother's sad reproachful eye,
A father's scowling brow—
But he may frown and she may sigh:
I will not break my vow!

I love my mother, I revere
My sire, but fear not me—
Believe that Death alone can tear
This faithful heart from thee.

IF THIS BE ALL

O God! if this indeed be all
That Life can show to me;
If on my aching brow may fall
No freshening dew from Thee;

If with no brighter light than this
The lamp of hope may glow,
And I may only dream of bliss,
And wake to weary woe;

If friendship's solace must decay,
When other joys are gone,
And love must keep so far away,
While I go wandering on,—

Wandering and toiling without gain,

The slave of others' will,
With constant care, and frequent pain,
Despised, forgotten still;

Grieving to look on vice and sin,
Yet powerless to quell
The silent current from within,
The outward torrent's swell

While all the good I would impart,
The feelings I would share,
Are driven backward to my heart,
And turned to wormwood there;

If clouds must EVER keep from sight
The glories of the Sun,
And I must suffer Winter's blight,
Ere Summer is begun;

If Life must be so full of care,
Then call me soon to thee;
Or give me strength enough to bear
My load of miscry.

MEMORY

Brightly the sun of summer shone
Green fields and waving woods upon,
And soft winds wandered by;
Above, a sky of purest blue,
Around, bright flowers of loveliest hue,
Allured the gazer's eye.

But what were all these charms to me,
When one sweet breath of memory
Came gently wafting by?
I closed my eyes against the day,
And called my willing soul away,
From earth, and air, and sky;

That I might simply fancy there
One little flower—a primrose fair,
Just opening into sight;
As in the days of infancy,
An opening primrose seemed to me
A source of strange delight.

Sweet Memory! ever smile on me;
Nature's chief beauties spring from thee;
Oh, still thy tribute bring
Still make the golden crocus shine
Among the flowers the most divine,
The glory of the spring.

Still in the wallflower's fragrance dwell;
And hover round the slight bluebell,
My childhood's darling flower.
Smile on the little daisy still,
The buttercup's bright goblet fill
With all thy former power.

For ever hang thy dreamy spell
Round mountain star and heather bell,
And do not pass away
From sparkling frost, or wreathed snow,
And whisper when the wild winds blow,
Or rippling waters play.

Is childhood, then, so all divine?
Or Memory, is the glory thine,
That haloes thus the past?
Not ALL divine; its pangs of grief
(Although, perchance, their stay be brief)
Are bitter while they last.

Nor is the glory all thine own,
For on our earliest joys alone
That holy light is cast.
With such a ray, no spell of thine
Can make our later pleasures shine,
Though long ago they passed.

TO COWPER

Sweet are thy strains, celestial Bard;
And oft, in childhood's years,
I've read them o'er and o'er again,
With floods of silent tears.

The language of my inmost heart
I traced in every line;
MY sins, MY sorrows, hopes, and fears,
Were there-and only mine.

All for myself the sigh would swell,
The tear of anguish start;
I little knew what wilder woe
Had filled the Poet's heart.

I did not know the nights of gloom,
The days of misery;
The long, long years of dark despair,
That crushed and tortured thee.

But they are gone; from earth at length
Thy gentle soul is pass'd,
And in the bosom of its God
Has found its home at last.

It must be so, if God is love,
And answers fervent prayer;
Then surely thou shalt dwell on high,
And I may meet thee there.

Is He the source of every good,
The spring of purity?
Then in thine hours of deepest woe,
Thy God was still with thee.

How else, when every hope was fled,
Couldst thou so fondly cling
To holy things and help men?
And how so sweetly sing,

Of things that God alone could teach?
And whence that purity,
That hatred of all sinful ways—
That gentle charity?

Are THESE the symptoms of a heart
Of heavenly grace bereft—
For ever banished from its God,
To Satan's fury left?

Yet, should thy darkest fears be true,
If Heaven be so severe,
That such a soul as thine is lost,—
Oh! how shall I appear?

THE DOUBTER'S PRAYER

Eternal Power, of earth and air!
Unseen, yet seen in all around,
Remote, but dwelling everywhere,
Though silent, heard in every sound;

If e'er thine ear in mercy bent,
When wretched mortals cried to Thee,
And if, indeed, Thy Son was sent,
To save lost sinners such as me:

Then hear me now, while kneeling here,
I lift to thee my heart and eye,
And all my soul ascends in prayer,
OH, GIVE ME—GIVE ME FAITH! I cry.

Without some glimmering in my heart,
I could not raise this fervent prayer;
But, oh! a stronger light impart,
And in Thy mercy fix it there.

While Faith is with me, I am blest;
It turns my darkest night to day;
But while I clasp it to my breast,
I often feel it slide away.

Then, cold and dark, my spirit sinks,
To see my light of life depart;
And every fiend of Hell, methinks,
Enjoys the anguish of my heart.

What shall I do, if all my love,
My hopes, my toil, are cast away,
And if there be no God above,
To hear and bless me when I pray?

If this be vain delusion all,
If death be an eternal sleep,
And none can hear my secret call,
Or see the silent tears I weep!

Oh, help me, God! For thou alone
Canst my distracted soul relieve;
Forsake it not: it is thine own,
Though weak, yet longing to believe.

Oh, drive these cruel doubts away;
And make me know, that Thou art God!
A faith, that shines by night and day,
Will lighten every earthly load.

If I believe that Jesus died,
And waking, rose to reign above;
Then surely Sorrow, Sin, and Pride,
Must yield to Peace, and Hope, and Love.

And all the blessed words He said
Will strength and holy joy impart:
A shield of safety o'er my head,
A spring of comfort in my heart.

A WORD TO THE "ELECT."

You may rejoice to think YOURSELVES secure;
You may be grateful for the gift divine—
That grace unsought, which made your black hearts pure,
And fits your earth-born souls in Heaven to shine.

But, is it sweet to look around, and view
Thousands excluded from that happiness
Which they deserved, at least, as much as you.—
Their faults not greater, nor their virtues less?

And wherefore should you love your God the
    more,
Because to you alone his smiles are given;
Because He chose to pass the MANY o'er,
And only bring the favoured FEW to Heaven?

And, wherefore should your hearts more grateful
    prove,
Because for ALL the Saviour did not die?
Is yours the God of justice and of love?
And are your bosoms warm with charity?

Say, does your heart expand to all mankind?
And, would you ever to your neighbour do—
The weak, the strong, the enlightened, and the
    blind—
As you would have your neighbour do to you?

And when you, looking on your fellow-men,
Behold them doomed to endless misery,
How can you talk of joy and rapture then?—
May God withhold such cruel joy from me!

That none deserve eternal bliss I know;
Unmerited the grace in mercy given:
But, none shall sink to everlasting woe,
That have not well deserved the wrath of Heaven.

And, oh! there lives within my heart
A hope, long nursed by me;
(And should its cheering ray depart,
How dark my soul would be!)

That as in Adam all have died,
In Christ shall all men live;
And ever round his throne abide,
Eternal praise to give.

That even the wicked shall at last
Be fitted for the skies;
And when their dreadful doom is past,
To life and light arise.

I ask not, how remote the day,
Nor what the sinners' woe,
Before their dross is purged away;
Enough for me to know—

That when the cup of wrath is drained,
The metal purified,
They'll cling to what they once disdained,
And live by Him that died.

PAST DAYS

'Tis strange to think there WAS a time
When mirth was not an empty name,
When laughter really cheered the heart,
And frequent smiles unbidden came,
And tears of grief would only flow
In sympathy for others' woe;

When speech expressed the inward thought,
And heart to kindred heart was bare,
And summer days were far too short
For all the pleasures crowded there;
And silence, solitude, and rest,
Now welcome to the weary breast—

Were all unprized, uncourted then—
And all the joy one spirit showed,
The other deeply felt again;
And friendship like a river flowed,
Constant and strong its silent course,
For nought withstood its gentle force:

When night, the holy time of peace,
Was dreaded as the parting hour;
When speech and mirth at once must cease,
And silence must resume her power;
Though ever free from pains and woes,
She only brought us calm repose.

And when the blessed dawn again
Brought daylight to the blushing skies,
We woke, and not RELUCTANT then,
To joyless LABOUR did we rise;
But full of hope, and glad and gay,
We welcomed the returning day.

THE CONSOLATION

Though bleak these woods, and damp the ground
With fallen leaves so thickly strown,
And cold the wind that wanders round
With wild and melancholy moan;

There IS a friendly roof, I know,
Might shield me from the wintry blast;
There is a fire, whose ruddy glow
Will cheer me for my wanderings past.

And so, though still, where'er I go,
Cold stranger-glances meet my eye;
Though, when my spirit sinks in woe,
Unheeded swells the unbidden sigh;

Though solitude, endured too long,

Bids youthful joys too soon decay,
Makes mirth a stranger to my tongue,
And overclouds my noon of day;

When kindly thoughts that would have way,
Flow back discouraged to my breast;
I know there is, though far away,
A home where heart and soul may rest.

Warm hands are there, that, clasped in mine,
The warmer heart will not belie;
While mirth, and truth, and friendship shine
In smiling lip and earnest eye.

The ice that gathers round my heart
May there be thawed; and sweetly, then,
The joys of youth, that now depart,
Will come to cheer my soul again.

Though far I roam, that thought shall be
My hope, my comfort, everywhere;
While such a home remains to me,
My heart shall never know despair!

LINES COMPOSED IN A WOOD ON A WINDY DAY

My soul is awakened, my spirit is soaring
And carried aloft on the wings of the breeze;
For above and around me the wild wind is roaring,
Arousing to rapture the earth and the seas.

The long withered grass in the sunshine is glancing,
The bare trees are tossing their branches on high;
The dead leaves beneath them are merrily dancing,
The white clouds are scudding across the blue sky

I wish I could see how the ocean is lashing
The foam of its billows to whirlwinds of spray;
I wish I could see how its proud waves are dashing,
And hear the wild roar of their thunder to-day!

VIEWS OF LIFE

When sinks my heart in hopeless gloom,
And life can show no joy for me;
And I behold a yawning tomb,
Where bowers and palaces should be;

In vain you talk of morbid dreams;
In vain you gaily smiling say,
That what to me so dreary seems,
The healthy mind deems bright and gay.

I too have smiled, and thought like you,
But madly smiled, and falsely deemed:
TRUTH led me to the present view,—
I'm waking now—'twas THEN I dreamed.

I lately saw a sunset sky,
And stood enraptured to behold
Its varied hues of glorious dye:
First, fleecy clouds of shining gold;

These blushing took a rosy hue;
Beneath them shone a flood of green;
Nor less divine, the glorious blue
That smiled above them and between.

I cannot name each lovely shade;
I cannot say how bright they shone;
But one by one, I saw them fade;
And what remained when they were gone?

Dull clouds remained, of sombre hue,
And when their borrowed charm was o'er,
The azure sky had faded too,
That smiled so softly bright before.

So, gilded by the glow of youth,
Our varied life looks fair and gay;
And so remains the naked truth,
When that false light is past away.

Why blame ye, then, my keener sight,
That clearly sees a world of woes
Through all the haze of golden light
That flattering Falsehood round it throws?

When the young mother smiles above
The first-born darling of her heart,
Her bosom glows with earnest love,
While tears of silent transport start.

Fond dreamer! little does she know
The anxious toil, the suffering,
The blasted hopes, the burning woe,
The object of her joy will bring.

Her blinded eyes behold not now
What, soon or late, must be his doom;
The anguish that will cloud his brow,
The bed of death, the dreary tomb.

As little know the youthful pair,
In mutual love supremely blest,
What weariness, and cold despair,
Ere long, will seize the aching breast.

And even should Love and Faith remain,
(The greatest blessings life can show,)
Amid adversity and pain,
To shine throughout with cheering glow;

They do not see how cruel Death
Comes on, their loving hearts to part:
One feels not now the gasping breath,
The rending of the earth-bound heart,—

The soul's and body's agony,
Ere she may sink to her repose.
The sad survivor cannot see
The grave above his darling close;

Nor how, despairing and alone,
He then must wear his life away;
And linger, feebly toiling on,
And fainting, sink into decay.

∽

Oh, Youth may listen patiently,
While sad Experience tells her tale,
But Doubt sits smiling in his eye,
For ardent Hope will still prevail!

He hears how feeble Pleasure dies,
By guilt destroyed, and pain and woe;
He turns to Hope—and she replies,
"Believe it not-it is not so!"

"Oh, heed her not!" Experience says;
"For thus she whispered once to me;
She told me, in my youthful days,
How glorious manhood's prime would be.

"When, in the time of early Spring,
Too chill the winds that o'er me pass'd,
She said, each coming day would bring
a fairer heaven, a gentler blast.

"And when the sun too seldom beamed,
The sky, o'ercast, too darkly frowned,
The soaking rain too constant streamed,
And mists too dreary gathered round;

"She told me, Summer's glorious ray
Would chase those vapours all away,
And scatter glories round;
With sweetest music fill the trees,
Load with rich scent the gentle breeze,
And strew with flowers the ground

"But when, beneath that scorching ray,
I languished, weary through the day,
While birds refused to sing,
Verdure decayed from field and tree,
And panting Nature mourned with me
The freshness of the Spring.

"'Wait but a little while,' she said,
'Till Summer's burning days are fled;
And Autumn shall restore,
With golden riches of her own,
And Summer's glories mellowed down,
The freshness you deplore.'

And long I waited, but in vain:
That freshness never came again,
Though Summer passed away,
Though Autumn's mists hung cold and chill.
And drooping nature languished still,
And sank into decay.

"Till wintry blasts foreboding blew
Through leafless trees—and then I knew
That Hope was all a dream.
But thus, fond youth, she cheated me;
And she will prove as false to thee,
Though sweet her words may seem.

Stern prophet! Cease thy bodings dire—
Thou canst not quench the ardent fire
That warms the breast of youth.
Oh, let it cheer him while it may,
And gently, gently die away—
Chilled by the damps of truth!

Tell him, that earth is not our rest;
Its joys are empty—frail at best;
And point beyond the sky.
But gleams of light may reach us here;
And hope the ROUGHEST path can cheer:
Then do not bid it fly!

Though hope may promise joys, that still
Unkindly time will ne'er fulfil;
Or, if they come at all,
We never find them unalloyed,—
Hurtful perchance, or soon destroyed,
They vanish or they pall;

Yet hope ITSELF a brightness throws
O'er all our labours and our woes;
While dark foreboding Care
A thousand ills will oft portend,
That Providence may ne'er intend
The trembling heart to bear.

Or if they come, it oft appears,
Our woes are lighter than our fears,
And far more bravely borne.
Then let us not enhance our doom
But e'en in midnight's blackest gloom
Expect the rising morn.

Because the road is rough and long,
Shall we despise the skylark's song,
That cheers the wanderer's way?
Or trample down, with reckless feet,
The smiling flowerets, bright and sweet,
Because they soon decay?

Pass pleasant scenes unnoticed by,
Because the next is bleak and drear;
Or not enjoy a smiling sky,
Because a tempest may be near?

No! while we journey on our way,
We'll smile on every lovely thing;
And ever, as they pass away,
To memory and hope we'll cling.

And though that awful river flows
Before us, when the journey's past,
Perchance of all the pilgrim's woes
Most dreadful—shrink not—'tis the last!

Though icy cold, and dark, and deep;
Beyond it smiles that blessed shore,
Where none shall suffer, none shall weep,
And bliss shall reign for evermore!

APPEAL

Oh, I am very weary,
Though tears no longer flow;
My eyes are tired of weeping,
My heart is sick of woe;

My life is very lonely
My days pass heavily,
I'm weary of repining;
Wilt thou not come to me?

Oh, didst thou know my longings
For thee, from day to day,
My hopes, so often blighted,
Thou wouldst not thus delay!

THE STUDENT'S SERENADE

I have slept upon my couch,
But my spirit did not rest,
For the labours of the day
Yet my weary soul opprest;

And before my dreaming eyes
Still the learned volumes lay,
And I could not close their leaves,
And I could not turn away.

But I oped my eyes at last,
And I heard a muffled sound;
'Twas the night-breeze, come to say
That the snow was on the ground.

Then I knew that there was rest
On the mountain's bosom free;
So I left my fevered couch,
And I flew to waken thee!

I have flown to waken thee—
For, if thou wilt not arise,
Then my soul can drink no peace
From these holy moonlight skies.

And this waste of virgin snow
To my sight will not be fair,
Unless thou wilt smiling come,
Love, to wander with me there.

Then, awake! Maria, wake!
For, if thou couldst only know
How the quiet moonlight sleeps
On this wilderness of snow,

And the groves of ancient trees,
In their snowy garb arrayed,
Till they stretch into the gloom
Of the distant valley's shade;

I know thou wouldst rejoice
To inhale this bracing air;
Thou wouldst break thy sweetest sleep
To behold a scene so fair.

O'er these wintry wilds, ALONE,
Thou wouldst joy to wander free;
And it will not please thee less,
Though that bliss be shared with me.

THE CAPTIVE DOVE

Poor restless dove, I pity thee;
And when I hear thy plaintive moan,
I mourn for thy captivity,
And in thy woes forget mine own.

To see thee stand prepared to fly,
And flap those useless wings of thine,
And gaze into the distant sky,
Would melt a harder heart than mine.

In vain—in vain! Thou canst not rise:
Thy prison roof confines thee there;
Its slender wires delude thine eyes,
And quench thy longings with despair.

Oh, thou wert made to wander free

In sunny mead and shady grove,
And far beyond the rolling sea,
In distant climes, at will to rove!

Yet, hadst thou but one gentle mate
Thy little drooping heart to cheer,
And share with thee thy captive state,
Thou couldst be happy even there.

Yes, even there, if, listening by,
One faithful dear companion stood,
While gazing on her full bright eye,
Thou mightst forget thy native wood

But thou, poor solitary dove,
Must make, unheard, thy joyless moan;
The heart that Nature formed to love
Must pine, neglected, and alone.

SELF-CONGRATULATION

Ellen, you were thoughtless once
Of beauty or of grace,
Simple and homely in attire,
Careless of form and face;
Then whence this change? and wherefore now
So often smoothe your hair?
And wherefore deck your youthful form
With such unwearied care?

Tell us, and cease to tire our ears
With that familiar strain;
Why will you play those simple tunes
So often o'er again?
"Indeed, dear friends, I can but say
That childhood's thoughts are gone;
Each year its own new feelings brings,

And years move swiftly on:

"And for these little simple airs—
I love to play them o'er
So much—I dare not promise, now,
To play them never more."
I answered—and it was enough;
They turned them to depart;
They could not read my secret thoughts,
Nor see my throbbing heart.

I've noticed many a youthful form,
Upon whose changeful face
The inmost workings of the soul
The gazer well might trace;
The speaking eye, the changing lip,
The ready blushing cheek,
The smiling, or beclouded brow,
Their different feelings speak.

But, thank God! you might gaze on mine
For hours, and never know
The secret changes of my soul
From joy to keenest woe.
Last night, as we sat round the fire
Conversing merrily,
We heard, without, approaching steps

Of one well known to me!

There was no trembling in my voice,
No blush upon my cheek,
No lustrous sparkle in my eyes,
Of hope, or joy, to speak;
But, oh! my spirit burned within,
My heart beat full and fast!
He came not nigh—he went away—
And then my joy was past.

And yet my comrades marked it not:
My voice was still the same;
They saw me smile, and o'er my face
No signs of sadness came.
They little knew my hidden thoughts;
And they will NEVER know
The aching anguish of my heart,
The bitter burning woe!

FLUCTUATIONS

What though the Sun had left my sky;
To save me from despair
The blessed Moon arose on high,
And shone serenely there.

I watched her, with a tearful gaze,
Rise slowly o'er the hill,
While through the dim horizon's haze
Her light gleamed faint and chill.

I thought such wan and lifeless beams
Could ne'er my heart repay
For the bright sun's most transient gleams
That cheered me through the day:

But, as above that mist's control
She rose, and brighter shone,
I felt her light upon my soul;
But now—that light is gone!

Thick vapours snatched her from my sight,
And I was darkling left,
All in the cold and gloomy night,
Of light and hope bereft:

Until, methought, a little star
Shone forth with trembling ray,
To cheer me with its light afar—
But that, too, passed away.

Anon, an earthly meteor blazed
The gloomy darkness through;
I smiled, yet trembled while I gazed—
But that soon vanished too!

And darker, drearier fell the night
Upon my spirit then;—
But what is that faint struggling light?
Is it the Moon again?

Kind Heaven! increase that silvery gleam
And bid these clouds depart,
And let her soft celestial beam
Restore my fainting heart!

DESPONDENCY

I have gone backward in the work;
The labour has not sped;
Drowsy and dark my spirit lies,
Heavy and dull as lead.

How can I rouse my sinking soul
From such a lethargy?
How can I break these iron chains
And set my spirit free?

There have been times when I have mourned!
In anguish o'er the past,
And raised my suppliant hands on high,
While tears fell thick and fast;

And prayed to have my sins forgiven,

With such a fervent zeal,
An earnest grief, a strong desire
As now I cannot feel.

And I have felt so full of love,
So strong in spirit then,
As if my heart would never cool,
Or wander back again.

And yet, alas! how many times
My feet have gone astray!
How oft have I forgot my God!
How greatly fallen away!

My sins increase—my love grows cold,
And Hope within me dies:
Even Faith itself is wavering now;
Oh, how shall I arise?

I cannot weep, but I can pray,
Then let me not despair:
Lord Jesus, save me, lest I die!
Christ, hear my humble prayer!

A PRAYER

My God (oh, let me call Thee mine,
Weak, wretched sinner though I be),
My trembling soul would fain be Thine;
My feeble faith still clings to Thee.

Not only for the Past I grieve,
The Future fills me with dismay;
Unless Thou hasten to relieve,
Thy suppliant is a castaway.

I cannot say my faith is strong,
I dare not hope my love is great;
But strength and love to Thee belong;
Oh, do not leave me desolate!

I know I owe my all to Thee;
Oh, TAKE the heart I cannot give!
Do Thou my strength—my Saviour be,
And MAKE me to Thy glory live.

IN MEMORY OF A HAPPY DAY IN FEBRUARY

Blessed be Thou for all the joy
My soul has felt to-day!
Oh, let its memory stay with me,
And never pass away!

I was alone, for those I loved
Were far away from me;
The sun shone on the withered grass,
The wind blew fresh and free.

Was it the smile of early spring
That made my bosom glow?
'Twas sweet; but neither sun nor wind
Could cheer my spirit so.

Was it some feeling of delight
All vague and undefined?
No; 'twas a rapture deep and strong,
Expanding in the mind.

Was it a sanguine view of life,
And all its transient bliss,
A hope of bright prosperity?
Oh, no! it was not this.

It was a glimpse of truth divine
Unto my spirit given,
Illumined by a ray of light
That shone direct from heaven.

I felt there was a God on high,
By whom all things were made;
I saw His wisdom and His power
In all his works displayed.

But most throughout the moral world,
I saw his glory shine;
I saw His wisdom infinite,
His mercy all divine.

Deep secrets of His providence,
In darkness long concealed,
Unto the vision of my soul
Were graciously revealed.

But while I wondered and adored
His Majesty divine,
I did not tremble at His power:
I felt that God was mine;

I knew that my Redeemer lived;
I did not fear to die;
Full sure that I should rise again
To immortality.

I longed to view that bliss divine,
Which eye hath never seen;
Like Moses, I would see His face
Without the veil between.

CONFIDENCE

Oppressed with sin and woe,
A burdened heart I bear,
Opposed by many a mighty foe;
But I will not despair.

With this polluted heart,
I dare to come to Thee,
Holy and mighty as Thou art,
For Thou wilt pardon me.

I feel that I am weak,
And prone to every sin;
But Thou who giv'st to those who seek,
Wilt give me strength within.

Far as this earth may be

From yonder starry skies;
Remoter still am I from Thee:
Yet Thou wilt not despise.

I need not fear my foes,
I deed not yield to care;
I need not sink beneath my woes,
For Thou wilt answer prayer.

In my Redeemer's name,
I give myself to Thee;
And, all unworthy as I am,
My God will cherish me.

My sister Anne had to taste the cup of life as it is mixed for the class termed "Governesses."

The following are some of the thoughts that now and then solace a governess:—

LINES WRITTEN FROM HOME

Though bleak these woods, and damp the
 ground,
With fallen leaves so thickly strewn,
And cold the wind that wanders round
With wild and melancholy moan;

There is a friendly roof I know,
Might shield me from the wintry blast;
There is a fire whose ruddy glow
Will cheer me for my wanderings past.

And so, though still where'er I go
Cold stranger glances meet my eye;
Though, when my spirit sinks in woe,
Unheeded swells the unbidden sigh;

Though solitude, endured too long,
Bids youthful joys too soon decay,
Makes mirth a stranger to my tongue,
And overclouds my noon of day;

When kindly thoughts that would have way
Flow back, discouraged, to my breast,
I know there is, though far away,
A home where heart and soul may rest.

Warm hands are there, that, clasped in mine,
The warmer heart will not belie;
While mirth and truth, and friendship shine
In smiling lip and earnest eye.

The ice that gathers round my heart
May there be thawed; and sweetly, then,
The joys of youth, that now depart,
Will come to cheer my soul again.

Though far I roam, that thought shall be
My hope, my comfort everywhere;
While such a home remains to me,
My heart shall never know despair.

THE NARROW WAY

Believe not those who say
The upward path is smooth,
Lest thou shouldst stumble in the way,
And faint before the truth.

It is the only road
Unto the realms of joy;
But he who seeks that blest abode
Must all his powers employ.

Bright hopes and pure delight
Upon his course may beam,
And there, amid the sternest heights,
The sweetest flowerets gleam.

On all her breezes borne,
Earth yields no scents like those;
But he that dares not gasp the thorn
Should never crave the rose.

Arm—arm thee for the fight!
Cast useless loads away;
Watch through the darkest hours of night;
Toil through the hottest day.

Crush pride into the dust,
Or thou must needs be slack;
And trample down rebellious lust,
Or it will hold thee back.

Seek not thy honour here;
Waive pleasure and renown;
The world's dread scoff undaunted bear,
And face its deadliest frown.

To labour and to love,
To pardon and endure,
To lift thy heart to God above,
And keep thy conscience pure;

Be this thy constant aim,
Thy hope, thy chief delight;
What matter who should whisper blame
Or who should scorn or slight?

What matter, if thy God approve,
And if, within thy breast,
Thou feel the comfort of His love,
The earnest of His rest?

DOMESTIC PEACE

Why should such gloomy silence reign,
And why is all the house so drear,
When neither danger, sickness, pain,
Nor death, nor want, have entered here?

We are as many as we were
That other night, when all were gay
And full of hope, and free from care;
Yet is there something gone away.

The moon without, as pure and calm,
Is shining as that night she shone;
But now, to us, she brings no balm,
For something from our hearts is gone.

Something whose absence leaves a void—

A cheerless want in every heart;
Each feels the bliss of all destroyed,
And mourns the change—but each apart.

The fire is burning in the grate
As redly as it used to burn;
But still the hearth is desolate,
Till mirth, and love, and PEACE return.

'Twas PEACE that flowed from heart to heart,
With looks and smiles that spoke of heaven,
And gave us language to impart
The blissful thoughts itself had given.

Domestic peace! best joy of earth,
When shall we all thy value learn?
White angel, to our sorrowing hearth,
Return—oh, graciously return!

THE THREE GUIDES

Spirit of Earth! thy hand is chill:
I've felt its icy clasp;
And, shuddering, I remember still
That stony-hearted grasp.
Thine eye bids love and joy depart:
Oh, turn its gaze from me!
It presses down my shrinking heart;
I will not walk with thee!

"Wisdom is mine," I've heard thee say:
"Beneath my searching eye
All mist and darkness melt away,
Phantoms and fables fly.
Before me truth can stand alone,
The naked, solid truth;
And man matured by worth will own,

If I am shunned by youth.

"Firm is my tread, and sure though slow;
My footsteps never slide;
And he that follows me shall know
I am the surest guide."
Thy boast is vain; but were it true
That thou couldst safely steer
Life's rough and devious pathway through,
Such guidance I should fear.

How could I bear to walk for aye,
With eyes to earthward prone,
O'er trampled weeds and miry clay,
And sand and flinty stone;
Never the glorious view to greet
Of hill and dale, and sky;
To see that Nature's charms are sweet,
Or feel that Heaven is nigh?

If in my heart arose a spring,
A gush of thought divine,
At once stagnation thou wouldst bring
With that cold touch of thine.
If, glancing up, I sought to snatch
But one glimpse of the sky,
My baffled gaze would only catch

Thy heartless, cold grey eye.

If to the breezes wandering near,
I listened eagerly,
And deemed an angel's tongue to hear
That whispered hope to me,
That heavenly music would be drowned
In thy harsh, droning voice;
Nor inward thought, nor sight, nor sound,
Might my sad soul rejoice.

Dull is thine ear, unheard by thee
The still, small voice of Heaven;
Thine eyes are dim and cannot see
The helps that God has given.
There is a bridge o'er every flood
Which thou canst not perceive;
A path through every tangled wood,
But thou wilt not believe.

Striving to make thy way by force,
Toil-spent and bramble-torn,
Thou'lt fell the tree that checks thy course,
And burst through brier and thorn:
And, pausing by the river's side,
Poor reasoner! thou wilt deem,
By casting pebbles in its tide,

To cross the swelling stream.

Right through the flinty rock thou'lt try
Thy toilsome way to bore,
Regardless of the pathway nigh
That would conduct thee o'er
Not only art thou, then, unkind,
And freezing cold to me,
But unbelieving, deaf, and blind:
I will not walk with thee!

Spirit of Pride! thy wings are strong,
Thine eyes like lightning shine;
Ecstatic joys to thee belong,
And powers almost divine.
But 'tis a false, destructive blaze
Within those eyes I see;
Turn hence their fascinating gaze;
I will not follow thee.

"Coward and fool!" thou mayst reply,
Walk on the common sod;
Go, trace with timid foot and eye
The steps by others trod.
'Tis best the beaten path to keep,
The ancient faith to hold;
To pasture with thy fellow-sheep,

And lie within the fold.

"Cling to the earth, poor grovelling worm;
'Tis not for thee to soar
Against the fury of the storm,
Amid the thunder's roar!
There's glory in that daring strife
Unknown, undreamt by thee;
There's speechless rapture in the life
Of those who follow me.

Yes, I have seen thy votaries oft,
Upheld by thee their guide,
In strength and courage mount aloft
The steepy mountain-side;
I've seen them stand against the sky,
And gazing from below,
Beheld thy lightning in their eye
Thy triumph on their brow.

Oh, I have felt what glory then,
What transport must be theirs!
So far above their fellow-men,
Above their toils and cares;
Inhaling Nature's purest breath,
Her riches round them spread,
The wide expanse of earth beneath,

Heaven's glories overhead!

But I have seen them helpless, dash'd
Down to a bloody grave,
And still thy ruthless eye has flash'd,
Thy strong hand did not save;
I've seen some o'er the mountain's brow
Sustain'd awhile by thee,
O'er rocks of ice and hills of snow
Bound fearless, wild, and free.

Bold and exultant was their mien,
While thou didst cheer them on;
But evening fell,—and then, I ween,
Their faithless guide was gone.
Alas! how fared thy favourites then,—
Lone, helpless, weary, cold?
Did ever wanderer find again
The path he left of old?

Where is their glory, where the pride
That swelled their hearts before?
Where now the courage that defied
The mightiest tempest's roar?
What shall they do when night grows black,
When angry storms arise?
Who now will lead them to the track

Thou taught'st them to despise?

Spirit of Pride, it needs not this
To make me shun thy wiles,
Renounce thy triumph and thy bliss,
Thy honours and thy smiles!
Bright as thou art, and bold, and strong,
That fierce glance wins not me,
And I abhor thy scoffing tongue—
I will not follow thee!

Spirit of Faith! be thou my guide,
O clasp my hand in thine,
And let me never quit thy side;
Thy comforts are divine!
Earth calls thee blind, misguided one,—
But who can shew like thee
Forgotten things that have been done,
And things that are to be?

Secrets conceal'd from Nature's ken,
Who like thee can declare?
Or who like thee to erring men
God's holy will can bear?
Pride scorns thee for thy lowly mien,—
But who like thee can rise
Above this toilsome, sordid scene,

Beyond the holy skies?

Meek is thine eye and soft thy voice,
But wondrous is thy might,
To make the wretched soul rejoice,
To give the simple light!
And still to all that seek thy way
This magic power is given,—
E'en while their footsteps press the clay,
Their souls ascend to heaven.

Danger surrounds them,—pain and woe
Their portion here must be,
But only they that trust thee know
What comfort dwells with thee;
Strength to sustain their drooping pow'rs,
And vigour to defend,—
Thou pole-star of my darkest hours
Affliction's firmest friend!

Day does not always mark our way,
Night's shadows oft appal,
But lead me, and I cannot stray,—
Hold me, I shall not fall;
Sustain me, I shall never faint,
How rough soe'er may be
My upward road,—nor moan, nor plaint

Shall mar my trust in thee.

Narrow the path by which we go,
And oft it turns aside
From pleasant meads where roses blow,
And peaceful waters glide;
Where flowery turf lies green and soft,
And gentle gales are sweet,
To where dark mountains frown aloft,
Hard rocks distress the feet,—

Deserts beyond lie bleak and bare,
And keen winds round us blow;
But if thy hand conducts me there,
The way is right, I know.
I have no wish to turn away;
My spirit does not quail,—
How can it while I hear thee say,
"Press forward and prevail!"

Even above the tempest's swell
I hear thy voice of love,—
Of hope and peace, I hear thee tell,
And that blest home above;
Through pain and death I can rejoice.
If but thy strength be mine,—
Earth hath no music like thy voice,

Life owns no joy like thine!

Spirit of Faith, I'll go with thee!
Thou, if I hold thee fast,
Wilt guide, defend, and strengthen me,
And bear me home at last;
By thy help all things I can do,
In thy strength all things bear,—
Teach me, for thou art just and true,
Smile on me, thou art fair!

I HOPED, THAT WITH THE BRAVE AND STRONG

I hoped, that with the brave and strong,
My portioned task might lie;
To toil amid the busy throng,
With purpose pure and high.

But God has fixed another part,
And He has fixed it well;
I said so with my bleeding heart,
When first the anguish fell.

Thou, God, hast taken our delight,
Our treasured hope away:
Thou bid'st us now weep through the night
And sorrow through the day.

These weary hours will not be lost,

These days of misery,
These nights of darkness, anguish-tost,
Can I but turn to Thee.

With secret labour to sustain
In humble patience every blow;
To gather fortitude from pain,
And hope and holiness from woe.

Thus let me serve Thee from my heart,
Whate'er may be my written fate:
Whether thus early to depart,
Or yet a while to wait.

If Thou shouldst bring me back to life,
More humbled I should be;
More wise—more strengthened for the strife—
More apt to lean on Thee.

Should death be standing at the gate,
Thus should I keep my vow:
But, Lord! whatever be my fate,
Oh, let me serve Thee now!

Printed in Great Britain
by Amazon